KINGDOM OF DREAMS

9 INTERACTIVE BIBLE STUDIES FOR SMALL GROUPS AND INDIVIDUALS

ANDREW REID AND KAREN MORRIS

SYDNEY · YOUNGSTOWN

Kingdom of Dreams
Second edition
© Andrew Reid and Karen Morris 2011

First published 1997

Matthias Media
(St Matthias Press Ltd ACN 067 558 365)
Email: info@matthiasmedia.com.au
Internet: www.matthiasmedia.com.au
Please visit our website for current postal and telephone contact information.

Matthias Media (USA)
Email: sales@matthiasmedia.com
Internet: www.matthiasmedia.com
Please visit our website for current postal and telephone contact information.

ISBN 978 1 921896 29 3

Cover design and typesetting Lankshear Design.

CONTENTS

How to make the most of these studies 5

STUDY 1: Getting some perspective
[Daniel 1:1-2] 9

STUDY 2: So… do you fit in?
[Daniel 1] 13

STUDY 3: Captains and teams
[Daniel 2] 21

STUDY 4: Into the fiery furnace
[Daniel 3 and 6] 29

STUDY 5: Who's the king round here?
[Daniel 4-5] 35

STUDY 6: The beast and beauty
[Daniel 7] 43

STUDY 7: Rams, goats, and lambs
[Daniel 8] 51

STUDY 8: Oh Lord, hear and act!
[Daniel 9] 57

STUDY 9: The awesome vision
[Daniel 10-12] 63

›› HOW TO MAKE THE MOST OF THESE STUDIES

1. What is an Interactive Bible Study?

Interactive Bible Studies are a bit like a guided tour of a famous city. They take you through a particular part of the Bible, helping you to know where to start, pointing out things along the way, suggesting avenues for further exploration, and making sure that you know how to get home. Like any good tour, the real purpose is to allow you to go exploring for yourself—to dive in, have a good look around, and discover for yourself the riches that God's word has in store.

In other words, these studies aim to provide stimulation and input and point you in the right direction, while leaving you to do plenty of the exploration and discovery yourself.

We hope that these studies will stimulate lots of 'interaction'—interaction with the Bible, with the things we've written, with your own current thoughts and attitudes, with other people as you discuss them, and with God as you talk to him about it all.

2. The format

The studies contain five main components:

- sections of text that introduce, inform, summarize and challenge
- numbered questions that help you examine the passage and think through its meaning
- sidebars that provide extra bits of background or optional extra study ideas, especially regarding other relevant parts of the Bible
- 'Implications' sections that help you think about what the passage means for you and your life today
- suggestions for thanksgiving and prayer as you close.

3. How to use these studies on your own

- Before you begin, pray that God would open your eyes to what he is saying in the Bible, and give you the spiritual strength to do something about it.
- Work through the study, reading the text, answering the questions about the Bible passage, and exploring the sidebars as you have time.
- Resist the temptation to skip over the 'Implications' and 'Give thanks and pray' sections at the end. It is important that we not only hear and understand God's word, but respond to it. These closing sections help us do that.
- Take what opportunities you can to talk to others about what you've learnt.

4. How to use these studies in a small group

- Much of the above applies to group study as well. The studies are suitable for structured Bible study or cell groups, as well as for more informal pairs and triplets. Get together with a friend or friends and work through them at your own pace; use them as the basis for regular Bible study with your spouse. You don't need the formal structure of a 'group' to gain maximum benefit.

- For small groups, it is *very useful* if group members can work through the study themselves *before* the group meets. The group discussion can take place comfortably in an hour (depending on how sidetracked you get!) if all the members have done some work in advance.
- The role of the group leader is to direct the course of the discussion and to try to draw the threads together at the end. This will mean a little extra preparation—underlining the sections of text to emphasize and read out loud, working out which questions are worth concentrating on, and being sure of the main thrust of the study. Leaders will also probably want to work out approximately how long they'd like to spend on each part.
- If your group members usually don't work through the study in advance, it's extra important that the leader prepares which parts to concentrate on, and which parts to glide past more quickly. In particular, the leader will need to select which of the 'Implications' to focus on.
- We haven't included an 'answer guide' to the questions in the studies. This is a deliberate move. We want to give you a guided tour of the Bible, not a lecture. There is more than enough in the text we have written and the questions we have asked to point you in what we think is the right direction. The rest is up to you.

5. Bible translation

Previous editions of this Interactive Bible Study have assumed that most readers would be using the New International Version of the Bible. However, since the release of the English Standard Version in 2001, many have switched to the ESV for study purposes. So with this new edition of *Kingdom of Dreams*, we have decided to quote from and refer to the ESV text, which we recommend.

6. Before you begin

We recommend that before you start on study 1, you take the time to read right through Daniel in one sitting. This will give you a feel for the direction and purpose of the whole book and help you greatly in looking at each passage in its context.

7. Suggestions for further reading

Because the book of Daniel is quite complicated in places it may be helpful to read a bit more widely. Andrew Reid, one of the authors of these Bible studies, has written an easy-to-read commentary on Daniel which may be helpful: *Kingdoms in Conflict: Reading Daniel Today*, Reading the Bible Today, Aquila Press, Sydney 1993.

GETTING SOME PERSPECTIVE

[DANIEL 1:1–2]

THIS FIRST STUDY IS DELIBERATELY short in order to allow you to get a feel for the context of the book of Daniel. The idea is that you read this introduction together and use the extra time to introduce yourselves, talk about how you will function as a group, spend some time praying, and so on.

If you are studying in a group, start with a large piece of paper (butcher's paper would be ideal) and draw a straight line with creation at one end and Jesus at the other.

On page 12 you will find a list of names, events and passages from the Old Testament. Photocopy the page and then cut out the pieces. Hand them around the group so that each person has a mixture of the pieces.

Go around the group and ask each person that has a 'name' piece to place it on the line at the appropriate place and to share with the group anything they know about the person. This is a whole group experience, so everyone can help. The aim is simply to get the names in some sort of order.

Once the 'name' pieces are on the paper, link up the events and passages with them, explaining how they connect with each other.

If you are studying on your own, draw lines on page 12 to connect the people with the correct passages and events. When you've done this, look up the Bible references to see if they help you place the people and events.

Creation   Jesus

WHEN GOD CALLS ABRAHAM IN Genesis 12, he promises Abraham three great things:

1. a land
2. that he will be a great nation
3. that he will bless him and cause him to be a blessing to all the world.

By the beginning of the book of Exodus, Abraham's children have indeed become large in number, but they are in captivity in Egypt and far from the land of God's promise.

The books of Exodus through to Joshua tell of how God rescues his people from Egypt, enters into covenant with them, and brings them into the land he promised Abraham. At first things go well and God rules his people directly through Spirit-filled leaders called 'judges' (see the book of Judges). However, the Israelites become unhappy with these sorts of leaders and ask God for a more steady sort of leadership such as a king would offer (1 Samuel 8). Although God considers that such a request really amounts to a rejection of his kingship over them, he allows the Israelites to have a king. He even makes an eternal covenant with King David, promising him that his children will always rule over God's people (2 Samuel 7).

Soon after David, the kingship fails and Israel is split into two: ten tribes in the north ruled by a series of various kings, and two tribes in the south ruled by the descendants of David. The ten tribes in the north turn against God and are eventually punished by him using the kingdom of Assyria. The two tribes in the south don't act any better, and eventually God judges them as well. This time it is by means of King Nebuchadnezzar, the King of Babylon. He overthrows them and carts them and their king (Zedekiah) off into exile. It is these events that set the context for the book of Daniel.

Read 2 Chronicles 36:5–10 and Daniel 1:1–2.

1. Describe the events recorded in these passages in your own words.

Read Psalm 137.

2. This psalm was written about the Israelites' experience of the exile. What does it tell you about the way the Israelites were feeling in exile? (If you want to do some more study on this, read the short book of Lamentations.)

» Give thanks and pray

* Thank God for being a just God who does not let sin—even the sin of his own people—go unpunished.
* Ask God for insight and understanding over the next eight studies as to what the book of Daniel means, and for the wisdom to know how to apply it to your situation.
* If you are studying in a group, pray for good relationships with each other so that you can gain the most benefit from the studies and be supportive of each other.
* Pray for opportunities to use what you learn in your conversations with other people.

People	Passage	Events
DAVID	1 Kings 8	Promise of return from exile
ISAIAH	Genesis 32:22-32	God's covenant promise
JOSHUA	Jeremiah 31:31-33, 27:22	Entry into the Promised Land
SOLOMON	Daniel 1	Temple established
DANIEL	2 Samuel 7:1-17	Creation
JEREMIAH	Deuteronomy 34:4-9	
ADAM	Isaiah 39:1-8	God's promise of the exile
ABRAM	Genesis 12:1-3	Kingship
MOSES	Genesis 2:15-17	Living in exile
JACOB	Exodus 6:6-8	Exodus

SO... DO YOU FIT IN?

[DANIEL 1]

EMACIATED, HOLLOW-EYED, AND despairing. Last night I watched again the photographs and black and white films recording the Holocaust. At times I'm tempted to think this was a dark part of human history that could never be repeated. But the strikingly similar photos of piles of skulls dug up after the exploits of Pol Pot, mass graves in Bosnia-Herzegovina, and cut up bodies in Rwanda show that our ability to wage war with gruesome violence and monstrous cruelty still remains.

These pictures are testimony to one of the difficulties any victorious side in war has with the vanquished. How should it handle the land and the people it has conquered? What should it do with the subjugated people? How can it retain its power over them?

1. List as many wars (ancient or modern) as you can in one minute.

2. When one nation defeats another, what are some of the methods used in dealing with the subjects and property of the conquered nation?

Read Daniel 1.

3. Of the various policies of war and conquest that you discussed above, which one does Nebuchadnezzar appear to be following?

4. What is Nebuchadnezzar trying to do?

5. What particular actions taken in this passage indicate that this is his policy?

THE OPENING VERSES OF DANIEL SET the context for the book. They tell us that the book is set on a global stage, involving whole nations. At the same time it is also set on a personal stage, involving particular representatives of those nations.

The global stage: Daniel 1:1–7

There are three telltale phrases in the first couple of verses of Daniel 1. These phrases pose very significant questions to which the rest of the chapter and even the rest of the book set out to respond. The first phrase tells us that "the Lord gave Jehoiakim king of Judah" into the hand of Nebuchadnezzar king of Babylon. In other words, it is God who has been at work to bring about this disastrous state of affairs with which the people of God find themselves confronted. He is active, but his activity has taken a strange turn in that it appears he has turned away from his people.

The second phrase tells us that Nebuchadnezzar not only defeated the Israelites but also took some of the articles from the temple of God in Jerusalem and "brought them to the land of Shinar, to the house of his god". The point is that not only has God apparently turned away from his people, but he also looks to have been devastatingly defeated. Surely no God who is really powerful would allow both his people and the symbols of his glory to be so demeaningly captured by other gods and their representatives.

The third phrase is less evident without some detailed knowledge. In verse 2, we are told that the articles from God's temple are deposited in the temple of Nebuchadnezzar's god in Shinar (or Babylonia). The reference to 'Babylonia' or 'Shinar' goes back to the tower of Babel in Genesis 11. The tower of Babel is a biblical symbol of human arrogance; of human kingdoms setting themselves against God's kingdom. By using this phrase, the author reminds us that Nebuchadnezzar is, in effect, setting himself against God.

Hence, after only two verses, we readers have a whole lot of questions running through our minds: Is God defeated? How is he going to deal with this situation? Will he take on the gods of Babylon? Will he demonstrate his power by rescuing his people? Will he do a Babel again? These verses and questions set the agenda for the book. It is a book about Babylon versus Israel, and the gods of the nations versus the God of Israel.

6. Imagine you were a young Jew in the exile. How do you think you'd react to the situation and to Nebuchadnezzar's actions?

To understand the stories of Daniel and his friends in Babylon, we need to understand some of the factors affecting them. Every Jew in Babylon knew why the Jews were there. Their ancestors had been given commandments by God, the first two of which were:

> "You shall have no other gods before me." (Exod 20:3)

and

> "You shall not make for yourself a carved image, or any likeness of anything that is in heaven above, or that is on the earth beneath, or that is in the water under the earth. You shall not bow down to them or serve them, for I the Lord your God am a jealous God, visiting the iniquity of the fathers on the children to the third and fourth generation of those who hate me, but showing steadfast love to thousands of those who love me and keep my commandments." (Exod 20:4-6)

These two commandments lay at the root of the Jewish faith, and at the root of their sin and their exile in Babylon. Because of their failure to keep these two commandments, the Jews were suffering judgement in exile. As a result of their sin in this area, they were experiencing God's anger and punishment, just as he had promised they would if they continued to sin (Lev 26:38-39; Deut 28:45-50; 1 Kgs 9:6-9).

This explains the resolve of Daniel and his friends. They were determined that they would not repeat the failure of their ancestors. They would be loyal and obedient to God and to his commandments at any cost. They would not jettison their identity as Israelites and as worshippers of the true and living God.

The personal stage: Daniel 1:8–17

7. Daniel accepted a Babylonian education and a name change, but then "resolved that he would not defile himself with the king's food, or with the wine that he drank". What could be wrong with the food and wine? (After thinking about this, see if the following passages help: Psalm 41:9; John 13:18.)

8. What statement is Daniel making by engaging in this act? For whose benefit is he doing it?

9. Why do you think Daniel is doing this, and why it so important to him?

10. How does God respond to Daniel's act?

The God who is present and active

THERE ARE THREE REFERENCES TO God's actions in the chapter. We have already seen the first one in verse 2, where we are told that it is by God's will and action that Israel finds itself in Babylon. The second occurs in verse 9, where God causes the chief of the eunuchs to show favour and sympathy to Daniel. The third reference comes in verse 17, where God acts to give "these four youths… learning and skill in all literature and wisdom".

Remember the first few verses? There was a markedly despondent tone. God looked defeated—he had handed his people over to a pagan king, and the vessels from his temple were deposited in the temple of Nebuchadnezzar's gods. The Babylonians and their gods undoubtedly had the upper hand.

However, by the end of the chapter things have changed completely. God has rescued Daniel, and the Babylonians and their gods have been shown to be no match for God and his people. As though to demonstrate this beyond any doubt, the writer concludes the chapter by telling us that Daniel survived until the first year of King Cyrus—the king who defeated the Babylonians.

God's means for defeating the Babylonians is not what we expect. We expect him to shatter Babylon with superior force of arms or devastating judgement like he did on the plain of Shinar back with the tower of Babel in Genesis 11. Instead the defeat comes through the determination of Daniel and his friends to resist assimilation, to be faithful to their God, and to take risks where necessary in preserving their identity as God's people.

» **Implications**

(Choose one or more of the following to think about further or to discuss in your group.)

- What is so important about being God's people?

- In what areas are our faith and identity as God's people put in jeopardy?

- What actions can we take to ensure that this identity is not taken away from us or put at risk?

- Where do you personally compromise your faith? What changes do you need to put into place that will help you remain faithful?

» Give thanks and pray

- Thank God for his sovereign power over the whole world. Thank him for preserving Daniel and his friends during the exile.
- Pray that Christians all over the world would understand the privilege and importance of being God's people, and would fight to hold on to that identity.
- Pray that God will be active as you make changes to your life, and ask him to help you remain faithful to him.

CAPTAINS AND TEAMS

[DANIEL 2]

NEBUCHADNEZZAR MUST HAVE been an awesome man to meet. He was born of a royal line and prepared for kingship from his birth. Even in his youth it was evident that he had inherited and even surpassed the considerable military skill and cunning of his father, Nabopolassar. When he became king, he continued and exceeded his father's program of military campaigns. Vast tributes were collected and huge numbers of captives were brought to Babylonia.

He was a reasonably good king at home. In keeping with his resolve, he dispensed justice, opposed hostile kings attempting to rob his regions of riches, reunited scattered fugitive people and made the whole land happy.

On top of this he engaged in massive building projects. He reconstructed the main river wall and quay, and began to plan a series of hydraulic works that would counter the eastward drift of the Euphrates. The palace he would build later in his reign would be magnificent. The upper walls would be decorated around with a band of blue enamelled bricks, the doors would be made of the best cedar, magan, sissoo or ebony wood and would be encased in bronze or inlaid with silver, gold and ivory. The doorway ceilings would be coated with lapis lazuli and the thresholds, lintels and architraves would be cast in bronze. Outside the palace there would be royal, terraced gardens housing a museum and looking out over the parkland.

Nebuchadnezzar was a very impressive man. It appeared that nothing could threaten or shake him. But then he had a very strange dream.

The world of dreams

The book of Daniel contains many references to dreams —dreams of Daniel, and dreams of people such as Nebuchadnezzar. In our modern world dreams are considered to be the gateway to an inner world. They inform us in visual language about repressed experiences and other processes of the unconscious. For the people of the ancient world, however, the realm of dreams was viewed very differently. Dreams provided a window into the world of the gods. To dream was to have a communication from the gods.

Archaeological digs in Babylon and Egypt have unearthed a large number of dream manuals. These manuals were often compiled by men sponsored by the rulers of the ancient world and contained long lists of dreams and their meanings. Once in possession of the content of the dream, the interpretation came easily.

Nebuchadnezzar knew this. For this reason perhaps he was glad that he could not recall his dream. Perhaps he thought that if there were someone who could present the dream itself, then they could be trusted to give a faithful interpretation. Alternatively, Nebuchadnezzar may have actually remembered the dream but hid it from his band of magicians and wise men so he could be sure of a true interpretation.

Read Daniel 2.

1. Divide the people in your group into two opposing groups. One group will represent Nebuchadnezzar and the Chaldeans. The other group will represent Daniel and his friends. (If you are studying Daniel on your own, just complete both sections separately.)

Nebuchadnezzar and the Chaldeans

a. List the attributes of the god/s this group believes in.

b. How do their gods act in the world?

c. How does this group think about other humans (including how they relate to each other and to the gods)?

d. Create a motto or slogan for Nebuchadnezzar and the Chaldeans that summarizes their overall approach to life and reality.

Daniel and his friends

a. List the attributes of the God this group believes in.

b. How does their God act in the world?

c. How does this group think about other humans (including how they relate to each other and God)?

d. Create a motto or slogan for Daniel and his friends that summarizes their overall approach to life and reality.

Come back together as one group and share what you found, making sure that you demonstrate where in the passage you got your information. Perhaps, in order to really get into the idea of opposing views of reality, each team could present its report in terms of "We believe..." rather than "The Chaldeans believed..." or "Daniel and his friends believed..."

Caught in cosmic conflict

IN DANIEL 2, WE SEE TWO VIEWS OF the world in conflict. On the one hand, there is Daniel and his friends. They knew they were in Babylon according to God's will (Dan 1:2). Moreover, they saw themselves as God's representatives. They represented a view of the world in which there was only one God, and he was the rightful ruler of all the world. But they didn't represent this view in a vacuum. They were surrounded by the best in ancient wisdom and learning and attitudes to things divine. Daniel and his friends were caught up in a conflict or contest between two kingdoms or world views.

However, when we read the chapter closely we see that both Daniel and his friends, and Nebuchadnezzar and his sorcerers, are representatives of their respective gods. The real contest is not between them but between the God of Israel and the gods of the nations.

» Implications

(Choose one or more of the following to think about further or to discuss in your group.)

- As Christians we too are God's representatives, surrounded by alternative views of God and the world. In what areas are these alternative views most obvious and clear? List some of the most common statements that represent these world views.

- Can you think of some more subtle ways in which the Christian world view is attacked? Write down some statements which demonstrate these. Discuss ways of responding to each of these.

- How should we react to this conflict? In what practical ways can we follow the example of Daniel and his friends, and take on the false gods of this world and show them up as counterfeit?

OF COURSE THE MAIN WAY WE TAKE on the false gods of this world and show them up as counterfeit is when we preach the gospel. When we share with other people the great news about who God is and what he has done in Jesus Christ, and they respond and accept him, God is saying clearly that he is still alive and active. He is still able to turn people away from idols to serve a living and true God (1 Thess 1:9).

This is also the case when we choose to live godly lives. Whenever we choose God's way over the world's, we demonstrate God's victory over sin, the world, the flesh and the devil, seen in the death of Christ.

Statues and images

Read Genesis 1:28, Jeremiah 27:4-7 and Daniel 2:37-38.

2. What are the similarities and differences between these passages? How does God view Nebuchadnezzar in Daniel 2?

3. What should be our attitude towards governments and other authorities? (See also Matthew 17:24-27, 22:15-22; Romans 13:1-7.)

4. In what specific situations do you think it might be appropriate to defy an earthly authority? (See also Acts 4:18-20, 5:27-32.)

In the ancient world a king would often set up statues or images of himself around his kingdom. These images represented the king and declared his rule. When God made humans he made them in his image; that is, he gave them his rule and authority (Gen 1:27-29; Psalm 8).

Daniel 2:37-38 clearly alludes to Genesis 1:28 (as does Jeremiah 27:4-7). The implication is that Nebuchadnezzar (and the nations that followed him) had been given dominion over God's world just as Adam had, to rule it as God's representatives.

The passage also makes clear that in the long run Nebuchadnezzar's kingdom looks like a huge idol. It is idolatrous—built by human hands and resting on feet of clay. Daniel 2 tells us that against such kingdoms God will finally set his own kingdom, carved out of a mountain (i.e. carved out of Mt Zion or Jerusalem —a Jewish kingdom), made "by no human hand", and eternal in its rule.

Such a kingdom became visible in history with the ministry of John the Baptist (Matt 3:2, 11-12). John the Baptist spoke in the same vein as Daniel, as he told people of a coming kingdom of God that would put an end to all the kingdoms of men and women. In Jesus—a son of David, a Jew— God would set up a kingdom made without hands that would never be destroyed. And wherever the gospel is preached, God is hurling the rock at the kingdoms of human beings. The day will come when he will do it one final, cataclysmic time, and on that day only his kingdom will remain.

›› Implications

(Choose one or more of the following to think about further or to discuss in your group.)

- If the only things and people left intact on the last day will be those that belong to God's kingdom as found in Jesus Christ, how will you fare?

- What needs to happen to ensure that you and your work survive on the last day?

- Are there ways in which you defy authority in government? What needs to change in your thoughts and actions in this area?

» Give thanks and pray

- Give thanks for Christians you know who faithfully stand firm in the face of those who attack the Christian world view. Ask God to give them perseverance, wisdom and grace.
- Pray these things for yourself as well.
- Ask God to help you by his Spirit with anything you noted under the final 'implication' question above.

INTO THE FIERY FURNACE

Children's stories?

IF YOU WERE TO WALK INTO ANY Christian bookstore and browse the shelves of the children's section, you would undoubtedly find a storybook about Daniel and his friends. Were you to delve into this book, past its bright colours and simple pictures you would probably find the story of Daniel in the lion's den or Shadrach, Meshach, and Abednego and the fiery furnace. It has always intrigued me that we modern Christians, who turn off our televisions so as to screen our children from violence, read these stories to our children before just about any others. Underneath it all, I suspect this is because we think these stories are too incredible for adults or are of no use to us.

Nothing could be further from the truth. The stories of Daniel and his friends raise some of the most complex issues of Christian faith. They talk about suffering and evil, and a good and powerful God who thrusts his saints into overwhelming and awful situations. They talk about maintaining faith in the face of severe testing. They talk about the presence and absence of God in a world that is seemingly dominated by forces more powerful and visible than God himself.

3²⁵ Fourth person
Son of God –
Jesus/Mesiah

Verses 16–18

The following alternative translation of these verses may help with this question:

"We do not need to make any response regarding this. If our God, whom we honour, exists, he is able to rescue us from the red-hot blazing furnace, and he will rescue us from your power, your majesty. Even if he should not, your majesty may be assured that we are not going to honour your gods or bow down to the gold statue which you have set up."[1]

Read Daniel 3.

1. Why do you think Shadrach, Meshach, and Abednego act in the way they do?

2. What does Nebuchadnezzar doubt (v. 15), and how do Shadrach, Meshach, and Abednego respond (vv. 16-18)?

3. What do the young men expect from God in this situation?

Daniel 3 and 6 present to us people who occupy positions of great importance in Babylon. They have wealth. They have position. They have status. At the same time they are people of great godliness. Can these truths about them coexist? Is it possible to serve the King of heaven while serving an earthly king? Is there a cost involved in serving two masters? And if there is a cost involved then who gets short-changed? To survive, do you have to compromise?

These are the questions that lie below the surface of the excitement and drama in Daniel 3 and 6. They are questions of crucial importance for God's people in any age, including our own as we live in a world set against God.

The cost and glory of discipleship

Christians throughout the ages have known two things to be true: on the one hand, God is the living God who alone makes sense of the world; and on the other hand the world is sinful, set against God, his purposes and his people. And so the Christian knows that living for God means inevitable trouble and persecution (2 Tim 3:12).

This is where the supernatural being in the furnace comes in. The important thing is not who that being is, but what God is saying through his presence. He is saying that whatever happens to the godly as they stand for him in a hostile world, he will be there with them. If we stand with him, he will stand with us.

Read Daniel 6.

Now go back and read verses 1-18. Stop there! We know what happens at this point, but the people involved didn't. Discuss together what it would have been like for each of them, using the following questions to guide your discussion:

4. Imagine you are the king. What might you be thinking and feeling at this point?

5. Imagine you are the officials. What might you be thinking and feeling at this point?

6. Imagine you are Daniel. What might you be thinking and feeling at this point?

7. At the end of the story Daniel and his God are vindicated, and God is praised. What is he praised for?

Don't miss the patterns!

THERE ARE SOME STRIKING PARALLELS between the story of Shadrach, Meshach, and Abednego in chapter 3 and that of Daniel in chapter 6. We could summarize these parallels under the following headings:

Belief in God costs something (Jas 4:4)

Choosing to believe in God means aligning ourselves with him and depending upon him. It means becoming a friend of God.

But there is a flip side. The world is set against God, its creator. Therefore becoming a friend of God means becoming an enemy of the world (and those who are in it), and since God is invisible and we are visible, the people of this world will often want to take out their grievances against God on us.

We can see this in both of these stories. The friendship that these young men had with God made them vulnerable, and such vulnerability cost them.

The presence of God is assured at all times (2 Tim 2:13)

One of the essential aspects of God's character is his faithfulness. God is true and faithful; he holds us in his hand. Once he commits himself to someone he doesn't let them go, nor does he allow anything to tear them out of his hand. Moreover, he promises that he will never leave us or forsake us no matter what happens to us. In Jesus he will be with us forever (Psalm 46; Matt 1:23, 28:20).

Again, although these young men didn't know Jesus, they knew that God would remain faithful to them. This is what their experiences were about.

God will vindicate himself and us

Because God is faithful and true he will always be victorious. He will always be finally vindicated. And since we have aligned ourselves with him, we will eventually be vindicated with him as we remain faithful to him.

The young men are demonstrations of this. They knew that God is true and they stuck with him despite huge temptations not to do so. Eventually, though through fire, they were saved. God vindicated them, and their oppressors recognized their integrity and the power of their God.

God will rescue

Again, because God is faithful and true he can never leave his saints. He can never be separated from them. Therefore he will eventually rescue them, as he did in both these passages.

The patterns we see in these chapters in Daniel have been seen many times in the Bible before (e.g. Joseph, the psalms of David, Esther, Jeremiah, etc.). We see them dramatically at work in the life, death and resurrection of Jesus. The faithfulness of God's people to him will always be taken advantage of, and will inevitably lead them into suffering and pain and eventually to vindication.

» Implications

(Choose one or more of the following to think about further or to discuss in your group.)

- Read 2 Timothy 2:11–13.

    - What principles could apply to the situations of the young men in Babylon?

    - Does God always rescue his people? If so, when? How? What from? If not, why not?

- Read Romans 8:37-39. How do these verses revise your answers to the above questions?

- What situations have you found yourself in where you think God should rescue you? What situations have you commonly heard Christians saying God should rescue them from?

- What does God promise?

- How do you feel about the fact that God may not always do what you want?

» Give thanks and pray

- Spend some time praying, telling God what you think and feel about these things.
- Thank God for his promises to us, and for guaranteeing them through Jesus.

Endnote

1. John Goldingay, *Daniel*, Word Biblical Commentary, vol. 30, Word Books, Dallas, 1989, p. 64.

WHO'S THE KING ROUND HERE?

[DANIEL 4–5]

THE FIRST RECORDED WORDS IN the public ministry of Jesus are those in Mark 1:15. Jesus says, "The time is fulfilled, and the kingdom of God is at hand; repent and believe in the gospel". From that moment on, nearly everything he says is coloured by language of the kingdom of God. This language of kings and kingdoms is the language of the book of Daniel more so than any other Old Testament book.

We've seen this ever since we opened the first page. The book is all about rule and authority, kings and kingdoms—kingdoms of humans and the kingdom or kingship of God.

Chapters 4 and 5 continue this exploration from a slightly different perspective by taking us into the lives, minds, and attitudes of two Babylonian kings. The main players are not God's people but foreign kings.

1. List the various people who have authority over you in the various aspects of your life.

2. How do you expect these people to act toward you in the exercise of their authority?

Not many parts of the Old Testament are written in the first person ("I, Alfred…"). Daniel 4 is the only case where it is a reasonably long bit of writing and from the lips of someone who is not an Israelite. Moreover, the form is that of a royal document of great authority.

The end result is that as we read Daniel 4 we get the feeling that what we are about to be told is very important, not only to its author but also for us (note that it is addressed to us in person—"to all peoples, nations, and languages, that dwell in all the earth"). Here is a pagan king addressing us and telling us what he has learnt about the true and living God.

Read Daniel 4.

3. List all the statements Nebuchadnezzar makes about himself. You could read them out loud to emphasize their impact.

4. List all the statements Nebuchadnezzar makes about God.

5. What picture do we get of the king from these statements?

6. What picture do we get of God?

7. What was Nebuchadnezzar's problem?

8. Why did God act in the way he did?

9. Which verse do you think gives the point of the whole chapter?

Statues and images again

BACK IN STUDY 3 WE SPOKE OF statues and images. In that chapter we noticed the remarkable similarity between the language used of Adam in Genesis 1:28 and the language used of Nebuchadnezzar in Daniel 2:37-38. Adam is in the image of God in that he is to rule over the world under God's rule and as God's representative. To be truly human is therefore to rule the world acknowledging:

1. that all rule is given by God (Dan 4:34-35)
2. that the rule needs to be exercised as God would exercise it—with kindness and no oppression (Dan 4:27).

This explains the incident where Nebuchadnezzar became a beast of the field. He stood on the roof of his palace—a place usually associated with arrogance, self-congratulation and sin (see 2 Samuel 11)—and said, "Is not this great Babylon, which I have built by my mighty power as a royal residence and for the glory of my majesty?" Here he was no longer living as a human should live before God. From God's perspective, Nebuchadnezzar was no longer seeing himself properly as a human being. It was as if he was insane and inhuman.

It also explains his return from being a beast. The transformation back to sanity and humanity came when "I, Nebuchadnezzar, lifted my eyes to heaven" and acknowledged that "*his* dominion is an everlasting dominion… *his* kingdom endures… *he* does according to his will… none can stay *his* hand or say to him, 'What have you done?'"

›› Implications

(Choose one or more of the following to think about further or to discuss in your group.)

- Remember back to our first study: the people of Israel were in exile; they were slaves to a foreign king. What impact would this story have had on them?

- What do you think was the author's purpose for including this story?

- This story is specifically addressed to us. What is its message for us?

- What difference does this story make to us?

Read Daniel 5.

10. Record the contrasts in the chapter using the following grid.

God	The gods

11. Record the contrasts between this chapter and Daniel 4.

Chaldeans and astrologers	Daniel

Nebuchadnezzar	Belshazzar

Read Mark 10:35–45.

12. How does Jesus exercise his rule, and what is that rule contrasted with?

Optional questions

- Read through Psalm 145 and list the characteristics of God's kingship.

Nebuchadnezzar vs. Belshazzar

CHAPTERS 4 AND 5 OF DANIEL are clearly linked in that they betray two approaches to rule. It is evident that there are good rulers and bad rulers. Rulers such as Nebuchadnezzar get things right when they humble themselves, acknowledge the overarching rule of God, and treat their subjects, God's things and God's people with respect. Bad rulers, such as Belshazzar, refuse to humble themselves, don't acknowledge the overarching rule of God, and don't treat their subjects, God's things or God's people with respect.

- Read Isaiah 52:13-53:12, which appears to be talking about a king-like figure. How does this king-like person exercise his rule?

Nebuchadnezzar learnt his lesson in chapter 4 but Belshazzar shook his fist wilfully at God and refused to learn from his predecessor's experience (Dan 5:18-23). He didn't give even a moment's thought to the God to whom he owed his existence, let alone his kingship. Pride goes before destruction and a haughty spirit before a fall (Prov 16:18; cf. Dan 4:37).

» Implications

(Do the first four questions below on your own.)

- Write down the relationships in which you have authority. How do you exercise your authority? Are you like God and Jesus, or Nebuchadnezzar or Belshazzar?

- In what areas do you fail to exercise authority in the way God expects?

- What specific things will you do differently now?

- How can others in the group help you, either in prayer or in practical support?

- If you are in a group, share what is appropriate from the questions above. Spend some time talking about how you can support each other practically and prayerfully.

» Give thanks and pray

- Praise and thank God for the way in which he exercises his kingship and authority.
- Either privately or in the group (if you feel comfortable to do so), spend some time repenting of any misuse of your authority and asking God for help and wisdom in your future use of it.
- Pray about the ways in which you plan to help each other in this as a group.

THE BEAST AND BEAUTY

[DANIEL 7]

Getting some perspective

The historical context

THE FIRST VERSE OF DANIEL 7 SETS the historical context for us—Daniel's dream comes to him "in the first year of Belshazzar king of Babylon". This is significant for a number of reasons. It was probably the year in which Cyrus took over the Median Empire on his way to the eventual overthrow of Babylon. While these were days of hope for many Israelites, it seems clear from chapters 10-12 (which largely arise in the last days of the Babylonian empire and the first days of the Median/Persian empire) that Daniel didn't share their optimism.

This is not very surprising given what Daniel had witnessed of Belshazzar's reign. Perhaps his unprincipled, arrogant, and rebellious reign caused Daniel to think deeply on questions such as, "What will happen when people like Belshazzar are allowed to go on? What will things be like when their persecution of God's people becomes unbearable? How can the people of God go on in a world where they are no longer rescued, where the flames consume them and lions tear them apart? If things do get worse, how can they be grappled with? How can God be explained? How can he be lived for in a world characterized by such fierce opposition?"

The literary context

The literary style of Daniel 1-6 is familiar to us and easy enough to interpret. The same can't be said for Daniel 7-12, so now is a good time to sketch in some background for our reading. The style of literature used in Daniel 7-12 has become known as 'apocalyptic' literature (from the Greek word 'apocalypse' meaning 'revelation'). This literature began to appear around the time of the Exile, and was composed in and for times of trial as a kind of private comfort for believers as they came to grips with the fact that things are not always all right on earth and that the people of God are not always victorious and kept safe.

As you read the Bible you will find pockets of apocalyptic tucked away in such places as the middle of the book of Isaiah (chapters 24-27) and in Mark 13 and 2 Thessalonians 2. Daniel 7-12 is the first full-blown expression of such literature. Other books of the Bible that are virtually completely apocalyptic are Zechariah in the Old Testament and Revelation in the New Testament. Some of the telltale features of this sort of literature are:

- strange imagery (e.g. beasts, dragons, angels)
- constant flipping between what's happening in heaven and what's happening on earth
- repetitive use of such numbers as 3, 3½, 4, 6, 7, 10, 12 and their equivalents (e.g. 3½ years is approximately 1260 days) or multiples
- dreams and visions
- reference to colours.

However, apocalyptic is not simply a literary style. It is also a philosophy of life and history—a world view. Fundamental to apocalyptic thinking was that history moves in regular, recurring patterns or waves of events, spiralling toward the point where God will finally burst in upon history in some dramatic way to wind up history, judge those in opposition, and vindicate those faithful to him. This is the world according to apocalyptic literature.

Many of us are familiar with some of the common ways of interpreting the apocalyptic literature of books such as Daniel and Revelation. People add up the years and try and make them fit various events in the past or the present, and then predict what will happen in the (usually imminent!) future. They examine various people or nations and attempt to demonstrate that Daniel or John had them in mind when they wrote.

Interpreting apocalyptic is not really a matter of adding up numbers and trying to see who in the modern world equals the figures in Daniel. Such an approach significantly misunderstands what apocalyptic is on about. It concentrates on one moment in history rather than doing what apocalyptic is doing—trying to show the 'big picture' of God's ways in the world. Apocalyptic says, "This is the way God always works in his world. Sure, it may get more intense towards the end of history but what happens then will be just like what's happening now, so don't be surprised by it."

Read Daniel 7.

1. If you feel adventurous, you might like to attempt to draw the scene portrayed! (This can be a very helpful way of trying to understand the passage).

2. Describe in your own words how you would feel if you were Daniel when you dreamt about:

- the beasts

- God

3. The beasts obviously represent the rule of various kings or kingdoms in comparison to the rule of God. List the differences between each.

The beasts	God

4. How does Daniel react to his dream?

Statues and images yet again

WE STARTED THE BOOK OF DANIEL by talking about a contest between the kingdom of God and human kingdoms. This has been a recurring theme throughout the book of Daniel, and it is related to humans being in the image of God. We could summarize the ideas like this:

- True human rule is exercised as Adam was meant to exercise it— recognizing it as a gift from God, and mimicking God's style of rule (just, merciful and kind).
- Rule that does not recognize it is delegated from God and does not mimic God's rule is no longer true human rule. It is inhuman or beastly.

This background is fundamental for understanding Daniel 7. The important thing is working out not who the various kings or kingdoms are but what the style of their rule is. The first beast has occasional human characteristics (like Nebuchadnezzar). However, the last beast with the little horn that springs from it has little true human rule left in it. This 'beastly' rule by four kingdoms is deliberately contrasted with the rule of the enigmatic "one like a son of man" (v. 13). The point is that this heavenly figure is also a human figure who exercises his rule in a truly human way (i.e. under the overarching rule of God). This 'son of man' is therefore a perfect man, one truly in the image of God—a new and perfect Adam.

Now that we've done this background and tried to understand what the term 'son of man' might have meant in its original context, it's time to do what we've wanted to do ever since we first read the term 'son of man': think about Jesus.

» Implications

* Why might Jesus have used the term 'son of man' to describe himself?

* Read Philippians 2:5-11. How does Daniel, and particularly Daniel 7, help us understand this passage?

WE HAVEN'T QUITE FINISHED WITH the term 'son of man' until we read the interpretation of Daniel's dream. In verses 1-14, the term 'son of man' clearly refers to one individual who does what no human being has done before—lives and rules as the image of God. As a result, he is given what Adam was given, but forfeited—the right to rule forever over God's kingdom. In verses 15-28, however, the rule of God is given "to the people of the saints of the Most High". Daniel 4 and 5 told us that God is the one who "rules the kingdom of men and gives it to whom he will". Although "whom he will" has first reference to the 'son of man' or Jesus, it does not stop there. Here in Daniel 7 and in other parts of the Bible, God speaks of other meek, humble, obedient human beings who have learnt to accept God's over-arching rule. And in Daniel 7, God promises that these people will inherit the earth (Matt 5:5).

Seeing the big picture

5. What was the situation of the Jewish people when Daniel saw the vision? (Refer to study 1 or read Psalm 137.)

6. What does Daniel 7 say about their future?

7. What do you think the purpose of recording Daniel's dream has for the people of Daniel's time and for those who followed?

8. What is the key verse of the passage? Why?

Victory assured

This is what Stephen sees in Acts 7. He has arrayed against him forces that are antagonistic to Jesus. He stands up for Jesus at great cost and as he is dying, God gives him an insight into heaven. He looks up and sees Jesus standing as the heavenly Son of Man, at God's right hand, ruling and judging on behalf of God, seeing Stephen's suffering and assuring him of victory.

THE PICTURE OF DANIEL 7 is grand. As we said earlier, it gives a philosophy of life and history. It tells us that in history there are anti-God forces that set themselves not only against God but also against his people. However, God is the king of the world. He is in control. He has always defeated and judged the forces of chaos and therefore his **victory is assured** in the future.

In addition, the saints of God should know that although things may get worse, there will be an end. God will send his ideal ruler. His coming and presence will begin the judgement process that will finally result in God's victory, the vindication of God and his saints, and the saints receiving a kingdom from God.

- Are there times in your life when you have felt completely overwhelmed by the way the world is going; the way things are going for you because of the forces at work in the world; the cost you have to pay for being a Christian? How does this passage encourage you as you face these circumstances?

- How do the life, death, resurrection and ascension of Jesus add to the message of Daniel 7 in this regard?

›› Give thanks and pray

- Thank God for the victory he has assured by the death and resurrection of his Son, Jesus Christ. Thank him for the comfort of knowing that "all dominions shall serve and obey him (Dan 7:27).
- Pray about the things that are overwhelming you at the moment. Ask for God's help in setting "your hope fully on the grace that will be brought to you at the revelation of Jesus Christ" (1 Peter 1:13).

RAMS, GOATS AND LAMBS

[DANIEL 8]

With Daniel 8 we move deep into apocalyptic literature. These chapters have traditionally been a fertile hunting ground for all sorts of weird and wonderful speculations about the possible course of history. Numbers have been counted and identifications made. In this study we have a much more modest but hopefully more helpful goal: to help you interpret this passage in such a way as to assist your approach to all such literature.

The first thing to notice is how the chapter begins. Up until now we have spent most of our time in Babylon, the capital of the Babylonian empire under such kings as Nebuchadnezzar and Belshazzar. In Daniel 8 the setting changes. Daniel is moved in his vision to Susa, the winter residence of the Persian kings. In other words, this vision concerns the next great force in world history as far as it affects God's people—the Persian Empire. Moreover, we are now in future time, far from the time of the exile of the Jews in Babylon.

The second thing to notice is that however strange the events are, the passage itself does provide some interpretation of those events. Verses 1-14 tell the story, and verses 15 and following give some interpretation of those events.

Read Daniel 8.

1. In the following table we have listed crucial elements of the story in verses 1-14. Write down the interpretation of those elements given in verses 15-27.

Vs	Event/Person	Interpretation	Vs
3	I raised my eyes and saw, and behold, a ram...		2a
3	It had two horns... *Strength + Power*	*Kingdom of Media + Persia*	20
5	...behold, a male goat came from the west... the goat had a conspicuous horn between his eyes.	*kingdom of Greece* *horn is Alexander the great.*	21 25
7	I saw him come close to the ram, and he was enraged against him and struck the ram and broke his two horns.		2c
8	Then the goat became exceedingly great, but when he was strong, the great horn was broken, and instead of it there came up four conspicuous horns...	*The Greek Empire would be divided into four parts.*	22
9	Out of one of them came a little horn, which grew exceedingly great toward the south, toward the east, and toward the glorious land.	*Greek king Antiochus*	23
10	It grew great, even to the host of heaven. And some of the host and some of the stars it threw down to the ground and trampled on them.	*will become strong will cause devastation destroy mighty + holy people.*	24 25
11	It became great, even as great as the Prince of the host. And the regular burnt offering was taken away from him, and the place of his sanctuary was overthrown.		25
12	And a host will be given over to it together with the regular burnt offering because of transgression, and it will throw truth to the ground, and it will act and prosper.		

God's patterns

Circles

ONE OF THE STRIKING THINGS ABOUT the Bible is that it is full of recurring patterns. These patterns become visible from the very early pages of the Bible. For example, the first chapter of the Bible tells us that God made the world and that it was very good. The second and third chapters tell us that humans don't like the rule of God. We prefer self-rule, which God allows us to exercise to our own detriment. However, the closing verses of the third chapter tells us that God's judgement on our self-rule is one of mercy and grace (he clothes Adam and Eve and puts them out of the garden in order to stop their state becoming permanent). This cycle of grace, sin, judgement, and grace is repeated time and time again in the first eleven chapters of Genesis.

Patterns like this keep recurring in the Bible, and the book of Daniel is no exception. In Daniel we have seen recurrent patterns of divine and human activity (remember the similarities we saw between Daniel 3 and 6).

The Bible appears to indicate that in God's world there are recurrent patterns of divine and human activity; given God's action, humans respond in characteristic ways, which in turn draws a characteristic divine response.

2. Read the passages and fill in the table.

	Isaiah 14:12–23	**Ezekiel 28:1–19**
The focus of the passage	The King of Babylon	The prince/ruler of Tyre
What is his chief sin?	Pride.	Pride.
What impact, if any, will he have on the people of God?		
How does/will God respond?	God will rise up against them 22/23	

	Daniel 8	2 Thessalonians 2:1–12
The focus of the passage	A king of bold face	The man of lawlessness
What is his chief sin?		*delighted in wickedness - v 12 oppose God v 4 + proclaim he is God.*
What impact, if any, will he have on the people of God?		*Will try to rule over distort counterfeit - v 9*
How does/will God respond?		*Lord Jesus will overthrow with breath of his mouth v 8*

As you can see, the patterns we see in Daniel 8 are not new. They have been seen previously and they will be seen again.

From beginning to end

The Bible tells us that God works not only in cyclical or recurrent patterns, but also in a line. The God of the Bible starts at the beginning and works toward a particular end he has in mind. He plans every event along the line with the end result in mind.

Apocalyptic: combining God's characteristic patterns

Let's have a look at these two patterns of God's activity. We could illustrate the first pattern with a circle that has a number of recurring points (e.g. God's grace, human sin, divine judgement, God's grace):

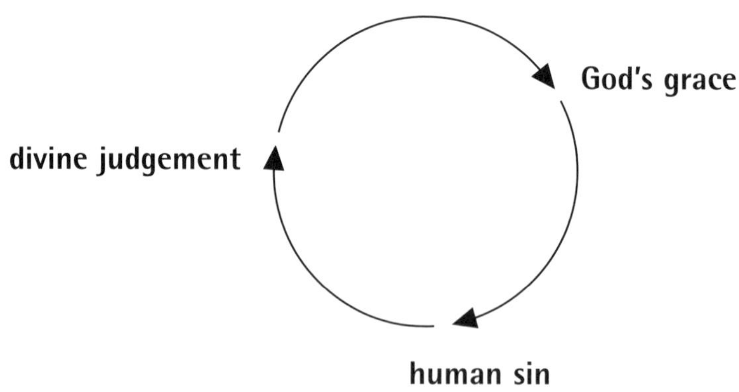

We could illustrate the second pattern with a line beginning at creation and progressing toward the end of history:

Apocalyptic writing appears to combine these two ways that God works in the world so that we get a sort of spiral towards that great climactic moment in history when everything will come to its ultimate expression as God intervenes to bring about the end of history.

Apocalyptic literature is therefore a bit like a section taken out of the spiral. It talks about a particular point in history and says that this is like a snapshot of where all history is going:

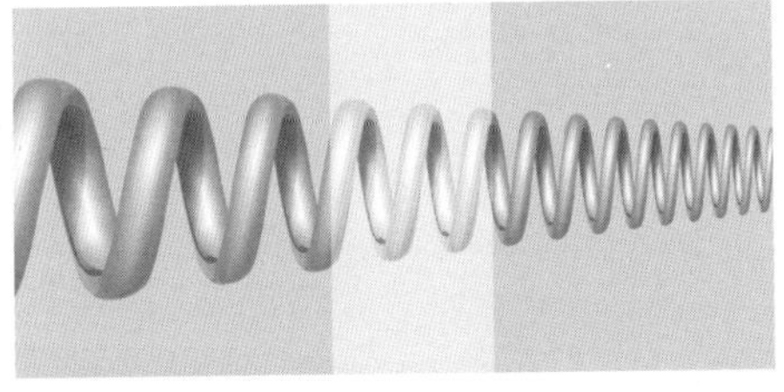

This is what is happening in Daniel 8. The events depicted here seem to refer to particular events in Jewish history. The ram represents the kings of Media and Persia (v. 20). The goat is the king of Greece (v. 21) from whom came four Greek kingdoms. The "king of bold face" (v. 23) appears to refer specifically to the reign of a king called Antiochus Epiphanes in the second century BC. In 167 BC this man—who believed himself to be the earthly manifestation of the Greek god Zeus—conquered Jerusalem and dedicated the temple in Jerusalem to his god ("the transgression that makes desolate"; v. 13). The reference to 2,300 evenings and mornings possibly refers to the time separating the appointment of a specific high priest through to the rededication of the temple in 164 BC (although it could also be an apocalyptic way of saying that there will be a fixed and limited period of time before God acts to vindicate his name and his servants, and that the sign of this will be the reconstruction of the temple).

If Daniel 7 is the broad canvas showing how God works in history and where he is headed, then Daniel 8 focuses in on one example of these forces at work and says that this will be the shape of the end of all history.

» Implications

Apocalyptic teaches us about the final end of those who set themselves against God and his kingdom. It tells us these truths in vivid language and cataclysmic images. The Bible also sets out the same truths in plain language, but it is the same message in the end. With this in mind...

Read 2 Thessalonians 1:3–12.

- What does God promise for those who don't know God and don't obey the gospel?

They will be punished with everlasting destruction. Shut out from the presence of the lord + from his majesty of his power (v 8+9)

- What does God promise for those who believe the apostle's testimony about Jesus (i.e. believe the gospel)?

counted as worthy of the kingdom of God. (v5) give relief to those who are troubled (v7)

- What can we expect as we wait?

Suffering - (v5)

- What sorts of things should we be praying for as we wait?

His purpose is fulfilled + every act prompted by your faith. (v11)

» Give thanks and pray

- Thank God for his righteous judgement, and for the relief he promises to his people "when the Lord Jesus is revealed from heaven with his mighty angels" (2 Thess 1:7).
- Ask God to keep giving you patience and wisdom as you study the book of Daniel.
- Spend some time praying about the things you noted above.

OH LORD, HEAR AND ACT!

[DANIEL 9]

Read Jeremiah 25:8–11 and 29:10–14.

1. According to Jeremiah, why were the Israelites in Babylon?

They didn't listen to God.

2. What had God promised to do after 70 years?

Punish the king of Babylon + his nation, the land of Babylonians, for their guilt – (Jer 25:12)
Jer 29:10 – I will fulfil my gracious promise to bring you back to this place.

3. What would be the stimulus for his actions?

Whole country will become desolation of Jerusalem.
Nations will serve king of Babylon for 70 yrs – (Jer 25:11)

How long?

The big question of the last chapter we studied was "How long, O Lord?" Given the presence of persecution, the question is not surprising from a personal point of view. But the question is far more than a personal one. When godly people ask God "How long?" they are doing so not only out of personal interest, but also out of concern for the glory of God. It is out of the same sort of concern that we pray, "Our Father in heaven, hallowed be your name"—which is fundamentally a cry for God to end the dishonouring of his name. In Daniel, it is also a cry for God to fulfil his word and bring an end to all usurpers to his kingship, in order that he alone might be king.

Perhaps it is the question of "How long?" that prompted Daniel to ponder the Scriptures "in the first year of Darius the son of Ahasuerus" (Dan 9:1). Darius is probably one and the same as Cyrus.[1] If this is right, then the first year of the reign of Darius/Cyrus would be an entirely appropriate time to be wrestling with prophecies about the return from exile, since prophets such as Isaiah had actually named him as the one who would be God's agent in bringing the people back to the Promised Land (e.g. Isa 44:28-45:13).

Read Daniel 9.

4. How does Daniel practise and describe praying?

5. What emotions are evident in his words?

6. List the descriptions of God.

7. List the descriptions of the people.

Sinned + done wrong
Covered in sham
not obeyed God
wicked
rebelled

8. If you are in a group, allocate the following verses around the group and have each person summarize the passage. Look for the essence of what is being said. Verses:

- 4-6

Repent + turned back to God

- 7-11

People are shameful + scattered because of
unfaithfulness to God.
Declaration of righteousness of God

- 12-14

fulfillment

- 15-16

Confession + forgiveness

- 17-19

Pleady with God - for mercy - hear prayes

Daniel's attitude in praying

As Daniel prays, a number of things about his attitude provide a helpful model for us in our prayer:

- He prays with seriousness, throwing his whole person into it: "Then I turned my face to the Lord God, seeking him by prayer and pleas for mercy with fasting and sackcloth and ashes"(v. 3).
- He acknowledges his solidarity with the people for whom he is praying: "*we* have sinned…" (e.g. v. 5).
- He prays as a representative and on behalf of his people (vv. 16-17).
- He prays on the basis of God's promises: God had promised to hear and forgive when his people humbled themselves and prayed on the basis of the temple in Jerusalem (2 Chron 6:36-39, 7:12).
- He affirms and acknowledges that God is righteous in all his actions (vv. 7, 14, 16).

9. What can we learn about the nature of Daniel's relationship with God from the prayer?

Submissiveness, repentance -

10. What does the prayer and God's response tell us about God?

merciful, forgiving just righteous

11. Why do you think this prayer is recorded in the Bible?

As an example -
that God does answer prayer

God's answer to Daniel's prayer

While Daniel is still praying to God, God sends the answer to Daniel's prayer through Gabriel. He comes to Daniel "in swift flight". Daniel's prayer is the prayer of the godly, and Gabriel assures him that "At the beginning of your pleas for mercy a word went out" (v. 23).

For us, God's answer is hardly enlightening at first sight but if we consider the context it becomes easier. The first half of Daniel's prayer focused on sin and the need for forgiveness. Verse 24 answers this part of Daniel's prayer and promises that sin and punishment will be done away with.

The second half of Daniel's prayer focused on the restoration of God's honour through the restoration of his people and his city. Whatever the numbers mean in verses 25-27, the main point of them is to assure Daniel that God is in control and an end to all the desolation and sacrilege is assured. At the appropriate moment God will cause his name, and the people who are called by his name, to be vindicated.

God is asking Daniel to understand that he is behind the processes of history and will not delay in answering the prayers of all those who long for forgiveness, justice, and an end to the dishonouring of God and the persecution of his people.

Every time we pray the Lord's Prayer, we line ourselves up with Daniel as we ask God to hallow his name and to bring in his kingdom. And through Daniel, God promises us that he will do it at the appropriate time.

For Daniel, Gabriel's answer must have been difficult. Daniel and his fellow Jews had waited all their lives for God to deal with Nebuchadnezzar. They had longed for the day of forgiveness, and atonement for the sins that had brought them into exile. The answer Gabriel brings is that, although there will be a return from exile, the day of realization of all of God's purposes is still a long way off. Eventually Daniel died without seeing the answer to his prayers.

>> Implications

(Choose one or more of the following to think about further or to discuss in your group.)

- How would you feel in Daniel's situation?

- Are you willing to not always see the answer to your prayers in this lifetime, and still believe in the God of history?

- What do (or should) you pray for that might not be answered in your lifetime?

- Read Hebrews 11. What does it say to people like Daniel and us about this problem of not necessarily seeing the answers to our prayers in this lifetime?

» Give thanks and pray

- Thank God for the "something better" (Heb 11:39) he has provided for us: the blood of Jesus Christ our Lord in payment for our sins so that we can be reconciled to him.
- Spend some time praying for the things you noted above, and ask God to give you patience in waiting for God's answers.
- Ask God to give you faith like that of Abraham, Moses and Daniel, and to keep you trusting in him until you come face to face with him.

Endnote

1. This is hinted at in the NIV footnote to 6:28, which notes that the translation can read, "Darius, that is, the reign of Cyrus". For further information, see the commentary suggested in the introduction.

THE AWESOME VISION

[DANIEL 10-12]

CHAPTERS 10-12 OF DANIEL BELONG together and concern one revelation given to Daniel. These chapters constitute the longest single section within the whole book, and many of the major details have already been seen in Daniel 8. On top of this, the details of these chapters seem very obscure to us—we are not sure who is being spoken about and where some of the places are and what is going on. Daniel 10-12 are difficult chapters to get your mind around, and to help deal with this we'll investigate it in a slightly different way.

In 10:14, we are told that the events depicted in these chapters concern "days yet to come" for the Jewish people. As it happens, they bear a striking resemblance to events from the second century that are testified to in Jewish and other reliable historical sources. In the section below we have outlined this story and placed beside it the verse references from Daniel so that you can read the history and then follow it through in Daniel.

1. Work through the following summary of the chapters, first reading the verses (in column 1) and then our summary (in column 2).

Verses	Summary
Dan 10:1, 12, 14	It is the third year of Cyrus, King of Persia, and Daniel is deep in prayer. In response to his prayers, God sends a messenger to instruct him and to outline for him future history.
Dan 11:2-4	The Persian kings of Daniel's time will be overthrown by a mighty Greek king, Alexander the Great (11:3). He will die early, leaving an empire to be divided among four generals. Two of the kingdoms that spring out of this division will become prominent—Egypt in the south (11:5) and Syria in the north (11:6).
Dan 11:5-19	These two kingdoms will war against each other, attempt alliances and act treacherously with each other. There will even be a time of peace between them. However, eventually a particular king in the north will be murdered.
Dan 11:20-28	His natural successor will be prevented from coming to the throne by the quick action of a usurper, Antiochus IV Epiphanes. This contemptible person will depose the current Jewish high priest and murder him, seizing rich lands and acquiring wealth. He will make two campaigns against Egypt and plot to destroy his nephew in the south.
Dan 11:29-32	He will also resolve to destroy all those in Palestine who are loyal to the covenant God made with his people. To this end, he will stop at the Holy City, Jerusalem, on his way back from Egypt and enter the temple and plunder its sacred treasures. His second campaign against Egypt in the south will bring him face to face with the Romans, who will stop him from waging war against Egypt. Fresh from this rebuff, he will decide to strengthen his rule at home through making his citizens fully Greek. This program will start with dissident Jews who have given up the covenant made by God with Moses. He will then act to stop the daily sacrifice in the temple, knowing that only faithful Jews will resist. They act as expected, resisting even under brutal persecution, pillaging, death and imprisonment. Nevertheless, persecution continues.

Verses	Summary
Dan 11:33-39	The faithful Jews are not rescued by divine intervention as Daniel and his friends had been, although they do receive a little help (perhaps through the encouragement of the first Judean guerrillas and activists). It is at this point that the picture painted by the angel becomes quite fuzzy and unclear to us. Like all those who step out from under the King of heaven's rule, this king will claim to be God, doing as he pleases. He will succeed, but only until God chooses to put an end to it.
Dan 11:40-45	Yet again the details become hard for us to understand. The messenger's telescopic lens focuses even more on the distant future, stating that there will be opposition and the falling of many nations. There will be an affront against the people of God and the land of God's people, a subsequent retreat, and the death of this one who sets himself against the King of heaven and against the people of the king of heaven.
Dan 12:1-3	In this last great battle there will be many deaths. The godly and ungodly will alike die. Together they will sleep in the dust of the earth and together they will awake from sleep to judgement. The wise, who have feared God and turned many to right relationship with the God of heaven, will awake to everlasting life. They will shine like the stars forever and ever. On the other hand, the godless—who have rejected the King of heaven—will wake to everlasting contempt and disgrace.

Imagine that you were a Jew in this time of persecution and trial. What are the questions you would want to ask God?

Note that although the numbers at the end of Daniel 12 can be figured in such a way as to fit various events at the time of Antiochus IV, this doesn't appear to be the main point. The main point appears to be that persecution will occur and will at time seem unlimited. Nevertheless, God does limit it, and the wise person, knowing this, should endure for that extra period. When the time has come, God will act to end persecution and deliver and vindicate his saints.

Read Daniel 12:4–13.

2. What questions does Daniel ask God's messenger?

3. What answer/s does Daniel receive?

The problem of suffering

Think about this passage and the whole book of Daniel and answer these questions on the basis of what the book says about God.

4. Does God care for his people and always have their best interests in mind?

5. Is God so great that he can do whatever he pleases whenever he pleases with whomever he pleases?

6. Does God allow his people to suffer, even to the point of death?

THE PROBLEM OF SUFFERING IS presented starkly in the book of Daniel. Most of us find it very difficult to reconcile a 'yes' answer to all of the above questions at the same time. We assume that if God was really good and great then he would not allow his people to suffer. Therefore when we come across his people suffering we come to one of a variety of conclusions:

- God is not really good. He doesn't always have our best interests in mind.

- God is not really great. He is not really in control of the world but is somewhat restricted by the actions of people in the world.
- The suffering is happening because we humans have not done some action that would have averted suffering.

But the Bible doesn't allow us to use any of these excuses. This is clear in Daniel. God is good; God is great; and God does allow his people to suffer.

So, how do we think about this? What

do we do? How do we answer our critics, let alone our own doubts and questions?

As Christians we must start at the right point. Rather than looking at the despair that we or our friends are suffering, we must turn to the centre of our faith—to the unjust suffering and pain of our Lord Jesus Christ. If we do this we will find a solid rock to stand on.

The first thing we find in the cross of Jesus is that God isn't detached from suffering. He is not remote and aloof, as he sometimes appears to be (notice that although he is said to be present with Daniel and his friends in their hour of need, we don't see many references to his immediate presence in Daniel 11). In the suffering of Jesus on the cross, God absorbs suffering into his own life. He experiences it from the inside. The end result is that he knows suffering as a fellow sufferer.

The second thing we find in the cross is that God isn't defeated or overcome by suffering. Jesus comes back from the dead. He is raised. God is indeed great and good. Wickedness brings suffering and death but God can bring life against these things and win. We see this also in Daniel 12:1-3. Evil appears to triumph in chapter 11, but in chapter 12 God rescues his people and vindicates them.

But the resurrection is not just vindication of God and his people. The resurrection of Jesus is also the first instalment of the new world—a world in which righteousness dwells and where suffering, pain, grief and death no longer exist. The point is that suffering cannot defeat God's good purposes for us. His great goodwill toward us is seen in the cross and will be vindicated at the last.

» Implications

- What *positive* features of suffering as far as God's people are concerned does Daniel 10-12 describe (if any)?

- Read Romans 5:1-5. What does this passage imply will be the normal lot of those seeking to live the Christian life?

- Read 2 Corinthians 4:7-12 and 4:16-18. What does this passage tell us about Paul's attitude toward the inevitable suffering that came upon him as an apostle? What positive features or outcomes from this suffering are there for him?

- When things are going badly for you because of your resolve to be a Christian, what is your first reaction? What have you learnt in this study that might change this reaction?

» **Give thanks and pray**

- Thank God for the book of Daniel and for what you've learnt from it over the last nine studies.
- Thank God for the reality to which his people look forward: a world in which righteousness dwells and where suffering, pain, grief and death no longer exist.
- Pray for those you know and love who don't know Jesus, and who have no hope of eternal life. Ask God to have mercy on them, and pray for opportunities and courage to share the gospel with them.
- Ask God to help you when you are struggling—either generally, or particularly for being a Christian—to remain firm in your faith and to keep your sights set on the relief you will one day experience in heaven.

Feedback on this resource

We really appreciate getting feedback about our resources—not just suggestions for how to improve them, but also positive feedback and ways they can be used. We especially love to hear that the resources may have helped someone in their Christian growth.

You can send feedback to us via the 'Feedback' menu in our online store, or write to us at info@matthiasmedia.com.au.

☸ matthiasmedia

Matthias Media is an evangelical publishing ministry that seeks to persuade all Christians of the truth of God's purposes in Jesus Christ as revealed in the Bible, and equip them with high-quality resources, so that by the work of the Holy Spirit they will:

- abandon their lives to the honour and service of Christ in daily holiness and decision-making
- pray constantly in Christ's name for the fruitfulness and growth of his gospel
- speak the Bible's life-changing word whenever and however they can—in the home, in the world and in the fellowship of his people.

Our resources range from Bible studies and books through to training courses, audio sermons and children's Sunday School material. To find out more, and to access samples and free downloads, visit our website:

www.matthiasmedia.com

How to buy our resources

1. Direct from us over the internet:
   – in the US: www.matthiasmedia.com
   – in Australia: www.matthiasmedia.com.au

2. Direct from us by phone: please visit our website for current phone contact information.

3. Through a range of outlets in various parts of the world. Visit **www.matthiasmedia.com/contact** for details about recommended retailers in your part of the world.

4. Trade enquiries can be addressed to:
   – in the US and Canada: sales@matthiasmedia.com
   – in Australia and the rest of the world: sales@matthiasmedia.com.au

Other Interactive and Topical Bible Studies from Matthias Media

Our Interactive Bible Studies (IBS) and Topical Bible Studies (TBS) are a valuable resource to help you keep feeding from God's word. The IBS series works through passages and books of the Bible; the TBS series pulls together the Bible's teaching on topics such as money or prayer. As of September 2019, the series contains the following titles:

Beyond Eden
GENESIS 1-11
Authors: Phillip Jensen and Tony Payne, 9 studies

Salvation Revealed
GENESIS 12-50
Author: Matt Olliffe, 10 studies

Out of Darkness
EXODUS 1-18
Author: Andrew Reid, 8 studies

The Shadow of Glory
EXODUS 19-40
Author: Andrew Reid, 7 studies

The One and Only
DEUTERONOMY
Author: Bryson Smith, 8 studies

Remember the Rock
JOSHUA
Author: Phil Campbell, 6 studies

The Good, the Bad and the Ugly
JUDGES
Author: Mark Baddeley, 10 studies

Famine and Fortune
RUTH
Authors: Barry Webb and David Höhne, 4 studies

God Will Have His King
1 SAMUEL
Author: Des Smith, 9 studies

Renovator's Dream
NEHEMIAH
Authors: Phil Campbell and Greg Clarke, 7 studies

The Eye of the Storm
JOB
Author: Bryson Smith, 6 studies

The Beginning of Wisdom
PROVERBS VOLUME 1
Author: Joshua Ng, 7 studies

Living the Good Life
PROVERBS VOLUME 2
Author: Joshua Ng, 8 studies

The Search for Meaning
ECCLESIASTES
Author: Tim McMahon, 9 studies

Two Cities
ISAIAH
Authors: Andrew Reid and Karen Morris, 9 studies

Kingdom of Dreams
DANIEL
Authors: Andrew Reid and Karen Morris, 9 studies

Burning Desire
OBADIAH AND MALACHI
Authors: Phillip Jensen and Richard Pulley, 6 studies

Warning Signs
JONAH
Author: Andrew Reid, 6 studies

Living by Faith
HABAKKUK
Author: Ian Carmichael, 5 studies

On That Day
ZECHARIAH
Author: Tim McMahon, 8 studies

Full of Promise
O.T. OVERVIEW
Authors: Phil Campbell and Bryson Smith, 8 studies

The Good Living Guide
MATTHEW 5:1-12
Authors: Phillip Jensen and Tony Payne, 9 studies

News of the Hour
MARK
Authors: Peter Bolt and Tony Payne, 10 studies

Proclaiming the Risen Lord
LUKE 24-ACTS 2
Author: Peter Bolt, 6 studies

Introducing Jesus
JOHN 1-4
Author: Matt Olliffe, 9 studies

Mission Unstoppable
ACTS
Author: Bryson Smith, 10 studies

The Free Gift of Life
ROMANS 1-5
Author: Gordon Cheng, 8 studies

The Free Gift of Sonship
ROMANS 6-11
Author: Gordon Cheng, 8 studies

The Freedom of Christian Living
ROMANS 12-16
Author: Gordon Cheng, 7 studies

Free for All
GALATIANS
Authors: Phillip Jensen and Kel Richards, 8 studies

Walk this Way
EPHESIANS
Author: Bryson Smith, 8 studies

Partners for Life
PHILIPPIANS
Author: Tim Thorburn, 8 studies

The Complete Christian
COLOSSIANS
Authors: Phillip Jensen and Tony Payne, 8 studies

To the Householder
1 TIMOTHY
Authors: Phillip Jensen and Greg Clarke, 9 studies

Run the Race
2 TIMOTHY
Author: Bryson Smith, 6 studies

The Path to Godliness
TITUS
Authors: Phillip Jensen and Tony Payne, 7 studies

From Shadow to Reality
HEBREWS
Author: Joshua Ng, 10 studies

The Implanted Word
JAMES
Authors: Phillip Jensen and Kirsten Birkett, 8 studies

Homeward Bound
1 PETER
Authors: Phillip Jensen and Tony Payne, 10 studies

All You Need to Know
2 PETER
Author: Bryson Smith, 6 studies

Rest Assured
1 JOHN
Author: Bryson Smith, 9 studies

The Vision Statement
REVELATION
Author: Greg Clarke, 9 studies

The Blueprint
DOCTRINE
Authors: Phillip Jensen and Tony Payne, 9 studies

Bold I Approach
PRAYER
Author: Tony Payne, 6 studies

Cash Values
MONEY
Author: Tony Payne, 5 studies

Sing for Joy
SINGING IN CHURCH
Author: Nathan Lovell, 6 studies

Woman of God
THE BIBLE ON WOMEN
Author: Terry Blowes, 8 studies